MEMO
SANDFIELDS

MEMORIES OF SANDFIELDS

Bethan Lloyd-Jones

THE BANNER OF TRUTH TRUST

THE BANNER OF TRUTH TRUST

3 Murrayfield Road, Edinburgh EH12 6EL, UK
P.O. Box 621, Carlisle, PA 17013, USA

ISBN-13: 978 0 85151 998 2

Typeset in 11.5/15 pt Sabon at
the Banner of Truth Trust
Printed in the U.S.A. by
Versa Press, Inc.,
East Peoria, IL

CONTENTS

Illustrations appear between pp. 61-62.

PUBLISHER'S NOTE

This vivid account was first published in 1983. It was widely appreciated. Reviewers found it delightful and absorbing reading, giving as it does a fresh perspective on the ministry of Dr Martyn Lloyd-Jones at the Bethlehem Forward Movement Church, Aberavon (popularly known as 'Sandfields') between 1927 and 1938.

Readers of the first volume of Iain Murray's biography of Dr Lloyd-Jones[1] will already have encountered several of the unforgettable characters described by Mrs Lloyd-Jones, and in some respects the present work can be regarded as a supplement to the biography, written by a uniquely-placed observer of the events of Dr Lloyd-Jones' first pastorate.

[1] Iain H. Murray, *D. Martyn Lloyd-Jones: The First Forty Years, 1899–1939* (Edinburgh: Banner of Truth, 1982).

All who have benefited from the ministry of Dr Lloyd-Jones, in person or through books or recordings, will be fascinated by this account of how some of 'the poor of this world, rich in faith' became 'heirs of the kingdom which God has promised to those who love him'.

THE PUBLISHER
May 2008

1

FIFTY YEARS AGO

December 1926, the month of his twenty-seventh birthday, saw the last of Martyn Lloyd-Jones' commitment to medicine. The London M.D. and the M.R.C.P. were behind him, and his term of research into Bacterial Endocarditis, funded by the Harmsworth family, had come to an end. It had been a turbulent year of ups and downs. In 1925 he had almost come to think that he had been mistaken about his call to the ministry, and he had plunged back into his research and medical work. But in 1926 the call returned with a power and insistence that he could not resist – nor did he want to.

When his decision was made known, everybody did their best to dissuade him – from fellow-doctors, family, friends, to his own minister! A remarkable exception was the weekly paper

John Bull which someone sent to me. Under the heading, 'From palpitations to pulpitations', it had a statement beginning, 'Dr Lloyd-Jones, a brilliant young heart-physician . . .', and under that, as comment: 'Hats off to Dr Lloyd-Jones'!

All this happened some twelve years after our first meeting in 1914. One Sunday evening, in the late summer of that year, I took my seat in the usual family pew in Charing Cross Road Welsh Chapel. In the seat in front sat a family I had never seen before. A very handsome, somewhat portly man with a beautiful head of greying wavy hair. Beside him sat his wife – smartly dressed and a good deal younger. With them three boys, the youngest next to his mother still wore his 'Eton' collar outside his coat. The middle one slight with straight black hair brushed across his forehead, and the third very like his father. In the after-meeting, their membership transfer papers were read out and they were received into the church, being introduced as the Lloyd-Jones family from Llangeitho.

The boys, Harold, Martyn and Vincent, were 15, 14, and 12! That was our first meeting, and I little thought . . . !

Martyn and I were engaged in June 1926, and I was proud to share with him those difficulties which followed his decision to leave medicine. By

December 1926 the storm he passed through had abated and people could see that their objections and pleas availed nothing. So in January 1927 we were married and after a short honeymoon and a dose of influenza (!) we went, in February, to Aberavon, South Wales, our first home and the scene of my husband's first pastoral charge.

I remember alighting from the train, in a grey drizzle, and being met by two or three people from the Church who soon whisked us away to the house of Mr and Mrs Robson where we had a royal welcome which warmed our very hearts. We stayed there for a week while the Manse was prepared for us and I look back with a grateful heart for all the help that Mrs Robson gave to me – she was truly a 'mother in Israel'.

At that time Aberavon was beginning to suffer from the great depression. Ramsay MacDonald was looked upon as an idolized hero and there were one or two years yet to run before the disillusionment set in when many a photograph of him was turned to the wall or put in the dustbin! There were bunches of lads on the street corners who had left school four or five years before, and had never had a day's work since. A general air of depression overspread the district.

Bethlehem Forward Movement Church, popularly known as 'the Forward' by its members, or as 'Sandfields', was a Mission or 'daughter Church' of the Presbyterian Church in the town and the older Church had representatives on the 'committee' which, in Sandfields, took the place of a diaconate. There was also quite a heavy debt, but a small membership.

When the books had been gone through, there were about ninety names that could be written in ink. These were warm and friendly people and kind to a degree. Nothing was too much for them to do for us, and we formed bonds that could never be broken. So began eleven-and-a-half happy, fruitful years, for which I will always thank God, and the 'daughter church', let me add, was soon of age, independent, and free of debt.

As I look back to that period, and to the beginning of my husband's ministry, there is perhaps one thing which stands out above all others in my memory. For readers to appreciate its significance I need first to mention a religious opinion very commonly held in the nineteen-twenties and thirties. It was often said by missioners, evangelists, and workers among youth that if young people were not converted in their teenage years there was little hope that they would be converted at all. This sentiment was so often heard that it was widely accepted.

I was a bit vague about it myself – I mean to say I was born into a Christian family, 'christened' as a baby, confirming the christening on becoming a church member at 12 years old, and so I did not know what else was needed. I was afraid of God, and afraid of dying, and eschewed evil because of this. I tried to do all a 'Christian' should do in such duties as church attendance and I accepted the Bible as the Word of God. But I had no inner peace or joy and I knew nothing of the glorious release of the gospel.

In those early years at Aberavon, I rejoiced to see men and women converted – drunkards, evil livers – all manner of types and backgrounds *and* all different ages! I rejoiced to see them and I envied them and sometimes wished, when I saw their radiant faces and changed lives, that I had been a drunkard or worse, so that I could be converted! I never imagined that *I* needed to be converted, having always been a 'Christian' or that I could get any more than I had already! In those first two years, God graciously used Martyn's morning sermons to open my eyes and to show me myself and my needs. I came to know my sins forgiven and the peace of God in my heart.

As for the age limit, there was no such thing: age did not matter. As the Church grew we were a mixture of every age under the sun, from

Georgie Sullivan, a teenage youth, to those near the end of life, the 'elderly babes' of our Church family. That is what they were, and that is how we thought of them.

Recalling their lives, I feel I understand the author of the Epistle to the Hebrews when he says, 'Time would fail me to tell of . . .' Of the wonders that we saw – among all kinds and conditions of men and women – I cannot tell all in these pages. I have confined myself rather to something I have always wanted to do, that is to put on record the stories of some of the 'elderly babes', especially those who, for one reason or another, I knew best. Their lives were indeed the final proof to me of the fallacy which would limit the grace of God to any period of life.

In addition to these outstanding memories I must also mention some of the particular features of church-life at Sandfields, the weekly prayer meeting and the Fellowship meeting and the annual Sunday School procession held every Whit Monday.

Before turning to these themes, however, I must tell the story of Georgie Sullivan, who, from the young end of life's scale, showed no less memorably the unimportance of age in the things of the kingdom of God. Georgie Sullivan came from a good solid Scottish-Northern

Irish family; his parents and sisters were faithful church members and Georgie was always at the Sunday School and the meetings. He was now fifteen and bright at school, really a very nice boy and popular with his own kind.

Then, suddenly, we heard that Georgie was ill. In under a week we all understood how ill – he had T.B. of the lungs in a virulent form. At that time, of course, everyone knew that the case was hopeless, for the wonder drugs were then unknown. There was much prayer, but Georgie was no better.

One Saturday night, Doctor[1] was very late home from the men's meeting – the Saturday-night Brotherhood. When he came he told a wonderful story. As he was about to leave the Church Hall, a message came – would he call at the Sullivans' house – Georgie was desperately anxious to see him. He went and found the boy in bed, with the typical hectic flush and shining eyes. He was very breathless, but, 'Doctor, please tell me what it is all about. I sit and listen to you and I know it is right, but I don't understand, I don't know what I have to do.'

---

[1] Throughout his ministry, both in Wales and later in London, Dr Lloyd-Jones was referred to affectionately as 'the Doctor' or simply as 'Doctor', to such an extent that it was used virtually as his name!

Martyn told him again, simply and plainly the way of salvation: Was he sorry for all the things he had done which were displeasing to God? He must tell God so and ask him to forgive him, and God would do so because the Lord Jesus Christ had paid the penalty for them on the Cross. They would be blotted out for ever, and he would be able to stand before God and know that he was forgiven and received to Glory.

Georgie looked in wonderment as he said, 'Doctor, is that really the whole gospel?', and Georgie's eyes were opened in time. He died that night, and died with a heart at perfect peace and full of joy. Fifteen or under, eighty or over, and any age and every age in between. Age is not a barrier.

2

WEEKNIGHT MEETINGS

The Church Prayer Meeting was held on Monday evenings at 7 o'clock. After a year or two it was always well attended, usually somewhere between 200 and 300 people being present.

The Minister would ask some one to begin with Bible reading and prayer. After a hymn, the meeting would be 'open' – no one was ever called or invited to pray. Doctor felt that the Holy Spirit would inspire and prompt, if we were humble and expectant. If he sensed a break after about half or three-quarters of an hour, he would give out a hymn, and then resume the meeting, and again bring it to a close in another half hour or so, when silence fell – always allowing a few minutes for the nervous or hesitant, in case they really wanted to pray.

These meetings were blessed beyond words – they were warm and sincere and we occasionally felt lifted to the very gates of heaven.

One such evening, Doctor had asked Harry Woods to open. He was a man in his sixties, I should guess, soundly converted from a decent hard-working ordinary kind of life, with not much thought for spiritual things. But when Harry Woods understood what was offered him in the gospel of Jesus Christ, he grasped it and gave himself to it, with all his being.

In his quiet way, Harry was remarkable, and I wish I could write of him in a manner worthy of my subject. But I never knew him well enough. He was shy and lived at the other end of the town; but he would often speak to Doctor and open his heart to him, especially on a Saturday night after the Brotherhood meeting.

He was different from most of the others in that he now seemed to see everything – even the most ordinary day-to-day things – in pictures and parables, and his accounts of these we found very moving.

There was an old wreck on Aberavon beach. A little coaling vessel – a collier – had failed to make the entrance to the docks, one stormy night long ago, and it had come to grief on the sandy beach, alongside the pier. There the wreck lay, an ugly blot on the scenery, but no one thought it worth while to remove it.

Harry Woods had some heart trouble and was not working. One day, as he was out walking along the beach, he stopped and stood gazing at the old wreck. Soon it was not the wreck that he saw, but his own ugly sinful heart and his old sinful life. And even as he looked through his tears, the swift tide came running in. Before his very eyes the wreck was covered and completely hidden from sight. Harry Woods saw – not the tide covering the wreck – but the precious blood of Christ hiding 'all his transgressions from view'! This was typical of the parables that he loved to tell Doctor on a Saturday night.

We always had a prayer meeting on Good Friday morning and I remember one especially. It was uplifting and quite outstanding. No one seemed to notice time and no one seemed to want the meeting to come to an end. Doctor stood at the door shaking hands as people left.

Harry Woods came along, and as he shook hands he said: 'Doctor, I'm going home a very disappointed man.' Doctor could hardly believe his ears. 'Why do you say that?' he said, 'didn't you enjoy the meeting, didn't you . . . ?' But Woods broke across his words, 'Doctor, I wanted to go to Heaven straight from the meeting, but it wasn't to be, and now I am just going home – I can't help feeling disappointed.'

A year or more after this, we were in the regular Monday-night prayer meeting and Doctor had asked Harry Woods to open the meeting. The Word came alive as he read, and then he prayed. He seemed to lead us to the very gates of Heaven and a kind of awe fell upon us, when Woods went to sit down.

As we bowed our heads again for the prayers of others, we heard a strange whistling breathing. It got louder and louder and then stopped, and we raised our heads to see two strong men catch Harry as he fell. They carried him out to the vestry. Doctor followed them as we sat, frozen in our seats. When he came back he told us that Harry Woods had gone to his eternal home in the Glory. None of us was surprised; he had seemed to be there already as he prayed.

Doctor prayed with us and we all went home sobered, amazed and thanking God for all we had seen and heard and felt.

The Doctor believed in interfering as little as possible in the prayer meeting. Very occasionally he would remind us of the purpose of it – that we should not be too personal, but remember that whoever was praying was, as it were, leading all the congregation to the Throne of Grace.

There would be half-guilty smiles when he told us it would be better in the public prayer meeting not to make mysterious references, and ask God to 'bless that person that I spoke to yesterday, who was in such trouble', and so on! 'It isn't necessary', he would say, 'and it breaks people's concentration on their prayers, while their minds go wandering off, wondering who the person was!'

Every now and then – not often, but just occasionally if he thought we were forgetting – he would tell us not to make long prayers. Many people wanted to pray and we must not be selfish with the time. That was, indeed, a word in season, for it was not unusual for thirty, sometimes more, sometimes less, to take a public part in the meeting.

There were other prayer meetings that stand out in my memory. We always believed, in every meeting, that the Lord was there – had he not promised that 'where two or three are gathered together in my name, I am in the midst'? We believed that – but there were two or three meetings where we *knew* it.

The night of Harry Wood's death was one of those times, when that wonderful sense of the presence of God enveloped us and all sense of time was gone, and God gave his people just a foretaste of Heaven, and the spiritual world was made very real.

The Fellowship Meeting was held on Wednesday nights, and, again, the hall was always well filled. Doctor would call someone to open the meeting with a hymn, reading, and prayer. Then he would ask if any had a question or problem they would like to discuss. 'Has anyone an experience to tell, or a question to ask, or a problem to discuss?', would be the usual words to open the discussion. Often the first offered would not encourage discussion, and he might himself give a brief answer and ask for other questions.

In this meeting he would not accept a purely theological question. This meeting must always deal with problems that affected Christian life and living. Once a question on these lines was asked, he would accept it for discussion, and sitting back in his chair, he would say: 'Well, what do you say to that?' Often he would open the question out to embrace a wide spectrum of related issues, and then guide the discussion through an hour, or an hour and a half, of points raised, thoughts shared, answers proffered, Scriptures quoted.

It was fascinating to see a whole congregation learning to think and weigh and attack a problem or question logically and biblically. I only realized what was happening to us on Wednesday nights when I went to many conferences, etc. and attended the same form of meeting. The contrast was interesting and revealing.

Now and again, in our Church meetings, there would be some very humorous interludes, and one thing always amused those of us who were hearers rather than talkers. Someone with strong opinions would rise to his feet and give an opinion in no uncertain terms, speaking perhaps a little dictatorially or dogmatically, and then as he was lowering himself back into his seat, the Doctor would say, 'Oh, Mr . . ., just a minute . . .', in the mildest way, and the poor man would find himself back on his feet and having to give reasonable, factual or biblical explanations of some of his original statements. What always caused the hidden smile and knowing look on the part of the congregation, was the look – the hunted look – on the man's face, when he realized that he could not get away with merely delivering a speech!

At the end of the discussion, Doctor would take ten or fifteen minutes to draw the threads together and sum up. Many would have liked to shorten the discussion and lengthen the summary! But he knew what was good for us and turned a stubbornly deaf ear to such suggestions!

So, we were learning without knowing we were learning, and we all loved it.

3

WOMEN OF THE CHURCH

Looking back over the years – over fifty of them by now – I cannot help wondering at myself, for I went to Aberavon without a qualm or a misgiving. I had never really thought about my position there. I do not think it was self-confidence – it was ignorance.

But soon after we were established and the introductory or welcome meeting was over, Mrs Bradley came to see me.

Mrs Bradley had been a working Sister with the Forward Movement – one of a devoted and faithful body of women who worked with true missionary zeal among the wives and mothers of the men working in the mining and commercial towns of North and South – chiefly South Wales. She had married a businessman and lived in

Aberavon. She was on the Church committee which served as a diaconate. She had started a Thursday afternoon Women's Meeting. And now she had come to hand the meeting over to the minister's wife – me!

Here commonsense and reason overcame panic. This was *her* meeting, I pointed out; she had started it and nursed it. She had had years of experience with such meetings, and I, not a day. She must carry on, and I would help her in every way I could. I won! It was a happy arrangement and I was gaining experience.

The Sisterhood was never a big meeting. The younger women and the girls were, for the most part, working and could not attend afternoon gatherings. But it was a warm fellowship and the speakers were carefully chosen, so that we could be sure that the Word of Life would always be spoken. The members were a cheerful company and, almost without exception, with a strong sense of humour. Their Christianity was very real to them and they loved to bring their unconverted friends along.

I remember only one awkward occasion in all the years. A missionary – a member of a sister church in the town – was on furlough, and I had heard that she was an excellent speaker, with a fascinating story to tell. We invited her and she came one afternoon to speak to us. All went well, until, while giving us an account of her own spiritual pilgrimage, she gave a vivid description of her husband and herself bidding good-bye to their – three or four – young children, as they left for the foreign field. She was graphic, and feeling that she had a sympathetic audience, she really gave a heart-rending picture of the farewell scene, the heart-broken children sobbing and crying with arms outstretched for 'Mummy, Mummy', while the train bore away herself and her husband, themselves stricken, but trying to bear up because they believed they were doing the Lord's will.

The result was not what she expected. The women's faces reflected their feelings. There was a stony, not to say belligerent, disapproval on every face and the meeting ended in a chill that could be felt. Some tried to thank the speaker as they left, but there was no heart in it, and I could hear mutterings: 'Better for her if she'd stayed with those children.' 'Why have them if you're not going to look after them?' 'Poor kids, what effect will it have on them?', etc., etc. I still don't know if she felt the ice, but I did, and I still remember the acute embarrassment of the situation.

Of course there were special friendships, but I was never conscious of cliques or sets amongst us, and they were all universally kind to the 'odd' ones. Oh! yes, of course, we had some. I would almost have grave doubts about a church which did not. Is there any other place where they can find such loving kindness and patient endurance?

In connection with this there was one interesting incident – nothing to do with the Women's Meeting, but in connection with these pitiful ones. A teenaged girl, very deeply disturbed, began to come to the meetings on Sunday. She always came early and sat right in the middle of the crowded ground floor. At some point, nearly always during the sermon, she would throw a fit, a typical epileptic fit to all appearances, and would have to be carried out – arms and legs flailing, eyes and head rolling and tongue hanging out – by two or three of the stalwarts. In the porch she would gradually recover, and, eventually, slip off home.

All this caused a real disturbance and the problem of what to do about it became acute. Then, one Wednesday night she came to the Fellowship meeting and sat in the very front row, a yard or two from where Doctor sat at his table.

Sure enough, about ten minutes into the discussion, Annie had a fit, violent and quite horrible to behold. Two or three of the men jumped to their feet, but, as they were about to advance upon her, Doctor put up his hand and waved them back. By this time the poor girl was on the floor and the hideous movements as violent as ever.

Doctor looked at her, and in a quite authoritative voice, said, 'Annie, stop that at once', and she stopped and was very still. 'Now, get up and sit quietly in your seat' – and again, she obeyed immediately and remained, quiet and perfectly behaved till the end of the meeting. 'It was a miracle', were the words on every tongue.

Was it? Was hers a true epilepsy, miraculously cured in that meeting, or was it the enemy – the devil – making use of that poor crazed girl's mind to spoil the work of God? If the latter, then the injunction in the Epistle of James was proved true before our eyes, 'Resist the devil, and he will flee from you.' In either case, we looked upon it as a miracle of grace and thanked God for it. We had no more disturbances. She would sometimes come and sit at the back of the church, but she was not cured, and eventually had to be put in safe-keeping for her own sake.

While on the subject of the 'odd' ones, I think that the strangest person I met in Aberavon, was the elderly lady with the eye-shade. She was not a member of the church but would sometimes attend on a Sunday evening.

One day, as I was walking to the town, I passed her house (quite unknowingly) and she was standing at the open door. She begged me to come in for a few minutes as she had something to tell me. I did not want to, for to tell the truth there was something strange and vaguely sinister about her, but I felt I could not refuse, and so I went in.

We sat in her 'parlour' – all very prim and tidy, as indeed, she was herself, with her white hair drawn back severely from her face, and dressed in her usual black with a white collar. She fixed me with her good eye and said, pointing to the eye-shade, 'I want to tell you about this.' I murmured something about being sorry, and was it a recent accident or something that had happened long ago . . . She broke across my poor attempt, and said, 'This was not an accident at all. I did it myself.'

I gaped at her. She went on, 'Christ says in the Bible that "if thy right eye offend thee, pluck it out and cast it from thee" – well, it did offend me and led me into sin, so I did that—' 'What . . . ?', said I, feebly. 'Yes, I plucked it out and cast it from me. Don't you think I did the right thing?'

How I wished Doctor had been there! I did my best and told her, that if she had only come to

Christ in repentance, and told him of her problem, he would have given her forgiveness and freedom, and his own strength to fight temptation, without her contemplating such terrible 'bodily exercise'. But she was not listening and did not really want to listen. I left her feeling I had failed her badly, but convinced that she was mentally unsound. When, later, I learnt that she had a bad reputation for loose living, I realized once more how the devil takes advantage of the mentally weak. They need our help and our prayers, and to be in a caring, understanding church.

But all this is a digression, let us return to our women's meeting. As we always had a speaker, there was no scope for the members themselves to do much speaking, but I often thought, as I looked around at them, that, almost without exception, each one of them would have a wonderful story to tell. Sometimes, indeed, the floodgates would open and we would find ourselves listening to the unburdening of a heart – sad, anxious, fearful, joyful. Whatever it was, there would be an equally heartfelt hearing and sympathy, not in the public meeting, but from some little group in the emptying hall, or on the way home.

The Sunday School was well-attended and lively, and like all Welsh Sunday Schools in those days, the ages ranged from babyhood well into the eighties. Doctor took the men's class, numbering between thirty and forty men of all ages. Mr Millard took the older women's class, while I had a class of young women with ages ranging from about eighteen to thirty. It was a new experience for me, but I found myself loving every minute of it. The girls really wanted to learn, they were not being forced in any way, they came of their own free will.

We chose our book for study, and then we went through it verse by verse. After reading a paragraph or passage – reading verse by verse in turn – each member was encouraged to start us off by asking a question on her verse. They would all talk and discuss and ask and answer questions freely. The time flew by. For some of them it was nothing new, they had always been to Sunday School from their childhood; but for others, newly awakened to spiritual things, it was a new world and they were enjoying having to think.

I remember one Sunday, someone raised the question of whether babies, dying in infancy, would go to Heaven. There was much talk, and many opinions. I was all for leaving such questions to the justice of our all-knowing and all-loving God, and for saying, like Abraham of old,

'Shall not the Judge of all the earth do right?'
Then one of the girls – speaking for the only time
that I can remember – spoke. She said: 'In the
Bible it says that Jesus said, "Let the little children come to me", and I think that if he said that
here on earth, he is still saying the same thing in
heaven now.'

Again, one Sunday, there was a certain restive
feeling (born, I am sure, of the prevalent political
trend) as we read the parable of 'the workers in
the vineyard' – the man who worked one hour
having the same wage as those who had worked
all day. They hesitated to say, in so many words,
that it was unfair – and yet! But when made to
look at it from the point of view of the poor
eleventh-hour workers being deprived of the joy
of working the whole day for such a kind and
generous master, there was a slightly guilty smile
and an admission of the spiritual truth behind
the story. And so we battled on, I learning with
them.

I must add one word on what having that class
did for me – it introduced me to the enjoyment
of biblical commentaries. I had been brought up
not to read commentaries. My father felt very
strongly about it. You must think for yourself
and compare scripture with scripture and use
your sanctified intelligence, and not read and

swallow other people's thoughts and ideas and teaching about the Bible, and so on . . .

So I had never read commentaries. But now I discovered something. If you are a member of a class, this procedure may serve a purpose. It may be an excellent spiritual exercise to use your own mind and train yourself to discuss and answer questions. But if you are leading a class, the more you read the better. So now I read commentaries. We had a good collection of them on all parts of the Bible, and I would read them all on the passage in hand, yes, and revel in them too, Welsh and English, the meditations of great men of God on God's Word.

I was thus enriched and far readier to meet the questions and demurrings of my class on Sundays. If there was disagreement over any point among the commentators, I would find my patient mentor in the study, and Doctor would always be ready to sort things out for me, reveal the real nub of the disagreement and give his opinion for me to take or reject. I need not say that I invariably took it, and was satisfied.

Some time in the early days – if I remember rightly it was towards the end of our second year – some of the women asked if we could have a Bible Class on an evening in the week. They approached Doctor about it, and he heartily approved, so long as the extra meeting did not keep anyone away from the regular church meetings – prayer meeting on Monday, and Fellowship meeting on Wednesday! No difficulty, they would come to them all, they reassured him, and he gladly gave his blessing to the proposal.

They were as good as their word, the regular church meetings suffered not at all, indeed some insisted that they were all the better for the Bible Class, and the Bible Class itself flourished. It was a mixture of all ages, and all eager to learn and study the Word. The new converts in particular greatly enjoyed this extra hour of Christian fellowship. We never had 'speakers' for this meeting. It was exactly like a Sunday School class on a larger scale, and there was real freedom for questions and answers, the recounting of some experience relevant to the subject under discussion, or the account of something heard or read with a bearing on it.

We did not hurry, or set ourselves a definite section to be dealt with in an evening. In about nine years or so, we worked our way through Genesis, Matthew, and Acts, and as far as the fourth chapter of Hebrews.

That was the point at which the Doctor and I left Aberavon for London and the wrench was like leaving one's family.

There was an incident in the life of Mrs Sullivan, Georgie's mother, that I am sure should be put on record, if only for the encouragement that some Christian people might receive by it. Mrs Sullivan and her husband were of good, sound, Scottish-Irish stock, and they had an ideal family life, not overburdened with this world's 'golden store', but comfortable and happy. Their daughter was our valued organist Always a God-fearing woman, as she sat under the new ministry for month after month, she found herself becoming more aware of spiritual things and more sensitive to them. One day she told me of a wonderful thing that happened in her life.

It seems that her one great treat and extravagance in life was the cinema. She could not bear to miss a change of programme, and this entailed a twice-weekly visit to the local theatre. And now she felt convicted – convicted that she was wasting her time and her money; and worse, the habit was sapping her interest in, and enjoyment of, spiritual things. So, she gave it up. She never spoke of it to anyone. She never tried to influence anyone else. It was a private problem of her own, and she solved it by promising God that she would give it up. Her peace of mind returned.

Then, one day, a friendly neighbour told her that a *very special* film was to be shown the following week; it was called *Damaged Goods*, and as the mother of a growing family she really should – in fact it was her duty – see the film for their sake. It would show her how to help them avoid the pitfalls which endangered the morality of growing children. Adamant at first, she confessed that the more she thought about it, the more she was shaken. So much so, that at last she gave in and promised to go with her neighbour to see the film during the following week.

The day came and the already disturbed and unhappy Mrs Sullivan, regretting her promise from the moment she made it, set out with her friend, but with a heavy heart. They got their tickets at the box office, and sat in their seats in the rapidly filling theatre. But at that point such a rush of remorse and distaste came over Mrs Sullivan, there in the theatre, sitting by her unsuspecting friend, that she sent up to heaven a desperate cry of despair and misery. She told me that her unspoken prayer was: 'Oh, Lord! please help me. I'm sorry I'm here, and if you can get me out of this situation, I will *never* be so foolish again.'

She felt a little better, a little less desperate now, but made no move to leave the cinema. Now it was time for the performance to start, a ripple of expectancy being felt all over the gathered audience. But as the curtain parted the manager stood there and made an announcement. Full of regrets and apologies, he explained that, unfortunately, something had gone wrong with the 'machinery' of the projector, and the film could not be shown that afternoon! Would all present call at the box-office on their way out and either ask for their money back, or *get a ticket for another date!!* Need I tell you which Mrs Sullivan elected to do? With a singing heart and a light step, she was soon outside and full of joy. Perhaps she did not know that her Father in heaven had said, 'Prove me now!' But then, who would ever think that God would answer prayer by putting a cinema projector out of action?

4

WHIT MONDAY

W hit Monday was a great day for the Sunday School at Sandfields, Aberavon. The weather forecasts, from the experts on 'wireless' and in the newspapers to the native pundits studying the clouds at sunset, were the subject of much discussion, and the cause of much hope or despair according to whether you were an optimist or a pessimist! But, either way, it was still a great day.

We met at the church door about two o'clock – the children and most of the adult members, too, for this was Wales and the Sunday School was for all who wanted to learn. There were classes for all ages – the men's about 40–50 strong, and always taken by the Doctor himself. So we were quite a gathering at the church door.

While we waited for the last stragglers to arrive, we formed ourselves into a procession, headed by Doctor and the solid block of men who walked with him. Each one of them would merit mention, were it possible. They were not all members – not yet, perhaps – but they were all drawn to the church and held as iron by a magnet.

'Tom Yank' was one of these. Somewhere in his sixties, he was a regular attender at the evening service and seemed to be held in this wonderful way. He was, by nature, a cynic. I cannot remember his real surname. The 'Yank' nickname was given him because he had spent some years working in America, and had come home with the evidence in his speech and accent! But he was certainly a cynic, and a sneer had almost become his usual facial expression.

One Sunday night, Doctor preached on Thomas the disciple – 'doubting Thomas'. On the following Wednesday night, we went along to the Fellowship meeting, happily certain that we were going to have a good meeting, but little knowing *how* good it was to be. The Minister's chair was set at a table, on a slightly raised dais, and we were all gathered round in a kind of 'square' semicircle. Tonight looked much like any other night's gathering, with the older men in the front row as near as they could get to the

Minister, and among them, as usual, was 'Tom Yank'.

After the opening of the meeting, during the short pause that usually followed, he got up and we all held our breath in wonder. He had never done this before, and we were riveted. I can see him now – short, stocky, with thinning grey hair and tanned weathered face. But – was it our imagination, or was there a subtle difference in that face? – a softer and less cynical look? Perhaps – but by this time he had begun to speak. At first he was obviously struggling with his natural reticence, and was breathless and hesitant, but as he went on, he seemed to forget all except what he wanted to tell us.

He confessed that, though he loved to listen to the preaching, and would feel, as he listened, that he wanted to believe, and to throw in his lot with us in church membership, yet, when the preaching was over, every doubt that Satan could rake up, would come crowding in on him, and he would leave without accepting salvation, and without coming into membership, and altogether feeling very miserable. But, last Sunday night, as Doctor preached on 'doubting Thomas', that sermon, he felt, could have been about him. He could identify with Thomas. He said that, at first, he could feel the bands of doubt like iron bars around his chest, so that he could scarcely breathe. But the story went on, and when Thomas, looking into the face of the risen Lord, cried out, 'My Lord and my God!', Tom Yank with his whole being said the same, and he felt the constricting bands around his heart melting away and they were gone for ever.

And now, here he was, shoulder to shoulder with Doctor in the Whit Monday march, as he had been before more than once, but this day he was a transformed man. The doubts and sneers were dispelled and in his heart was the certain knowledge that if they ever showed their face again, he would know how to deal with them.

But, to return to our Whit Monday – the procession soon took shape and set out. First a solid phalanx of men, followed by the women, with the children, dozens of them with guardian teachers and mothers, aunts and big sisters, bringing up the rear. Every little girl had a new dress for Whitsun – worn with the dash and confidence of a little girl in a new dress! Even the boys tolerated a certain degree of dressing up.

Thus we set off in good order, singing as we went, 'Onward! Christian Soldiers' and 'Who is on the Lord's side?', or 'Stand up, Stand up for Jesus'. We marched through all the streets of our district, passing the homes of the children as we went, happy to see some members of their families standing at the doors and waving to the enthusiastic little singers as they went by! Problems? Oh, of course! usually only two.

The one was *tar*. The Town Council in its wisdom always tarred the roads the week before Whitsun, with devastating effects on new dresses and little white shoes! In time we learned how to dodge the worst of it, but it was certainly a problem.

The second problem was in the nature and build-up of the procession itself. The men set the pace – a good steady walking pace – fine! But what they did not realize was that a steady pace for the head of the procession, meant that when it came to half-way along, the women had to quicken their pace to keep up, and when it came to the tail end, the children with their teachers were having to run or be left behind. A message was sent to the front, 'Slow down, please.' But the men could never appreciate the situation! After all, they were going at funeral pace already!

It was all great fun for the children and they loved it. We, for our part, were happy for them and hoped and prayed that the whole exercise was part of the church's call to be a witness to the world, as the hymn-writer puts it:

. . . A lamp of burning gold,
To bear before the nations
Thy true light as of old . . .

Then we returned to the church hall, and at that point the weather became important and effectively directed the course of the afternoon's activities. A fine day would see the whole contingent making for the sand-dunes. But, before they left, the mothers were there, rounding up their offspring, and exchanging the new little 'best dresses' for last year's summer cottons, more suitable for games and races!

The sand-dunes, lying between town and sea-front, stretched for miles along this part of the Welsh coast. Indeed, the extension of the old town of Aberavon, known as Sandfields, is built on sandy ground cleared of the dunes, and new roads with rows of houses encroached on the dunes, as they were needed. 'Building on sand is all right so long as you have good solid foundations,' said one of the planners of the new manse to me. 'It's the foundations that matter.'

I remember a member of the church committee, introducing us to the district and pointing out places of interest, saying to us, 'This is the third Aberavon, you know.' 'Where are the other two?' said I. 'Under there' (pointing to the ground beneath our feet) 'that is, what wasn't washed away.' I confess that his words did come to my mind sometimes, when I lay awake at night and heard the pounding of the waves on the beach, as the south-westerly gales swept the spring tide up the Bristol Channel! But there was one spot among the dunes, well known to the Sunday School teachers and scholars, which was ideal for games and races. On a lovely afternoon, that is where the procession, now a flock of excited youngsters and their teachers, could be seen heading. It was a large open space, surrounded by the sand-dunes, which made good vantage points for sitting down in comfort and seeing everything at the same time.

These dunes also proved to be a tremendous asset in other ways. Doctor would be sitting, relaxed and unoccupied as it were, and many, too shy to approach him in the vestry, would stop to get to know him, and get known by him. Often it might be just a pleasant conversation in general, or about the significance of current events. It all helped; but sometimes, hearts were opened and a work done for eternity, in the spring sunshine on the sand-dunes.

Edgar came into the latter category. He was a spry, wiry, smallish man, with a good position on the Docks. He was interested in politics and a near-worshipper of Ramsay MacDonald. But he had also been showing interest in the work at 'The Forward', as our church continued to be called. He had started coming sporadically to the evening service. His great trouble and problem was drink, and his place of work – the docks – was no help to him in this. Coaling vessels and Scandinavian vessels bringing pit-props for the mines had Captains who were glad to show their appreciation by giving drinks, and presents of wine, and so on, to take home.

When Edgar was seen, sitting beside Doctor on their sandy grandstand, deep in conversation, hopes ran high, and, indeed, that day was the turning-point in his life. His problem was dealt with, his need was met, and he rejoiced in his salvation. At a later date he became ill, and Doctor went to see him. He lay in bed. Facing him hung Ramsay MacDonald's photograph with its face turned to the wall. Edgar drew Doctor's attention to a series of three enlarged snapshots in a place of honour, each with a caption:

1. Edgar dishevelled and down-at-heel and very drunk, clinging to a lamp post. Caption: *Lost*.

2. Edgar, sitting, talking to the Doctor on the sand dune. Caption: *Found*.

3. Edgar, immaculate in a uniform-type suit, alert and clean-looking, with peace and contentment lighting up his face. Caption: *Saved.*

But, once more to return to Whit Monday: what if it turned out to be a wet afternoon, as well it might be, with the south-westerly gales blowing the drenching rain horizontally into our faces? No problem! In that case, we were all herded into the chapel, and we filled it from door to pulpit and from floor to ceiling. Then, for a couple of hours or more – indeed, until the word came from the kitchen that tea was ready, we all enjoyed a first-rate impromptu concert. There was an abundance of talent in all age groups, and some really beautiful voices. I was told that I had missed the 'star turn' by going to help in the kitchen – this was Doctor singing one of the old favourite hymns in a quartet. He could read the part – bass for him – easily and well, given the sol-fa, and not the old notation!

It was in this gathering always, that the church secretary came into his own. He was in his element with children, and could keep them enthralled, even hundreds of them at a time, with stories and knowing little jokes. He never failed to get responses from them if he should throw questions at them as he spoke; in fact, he could do what he liked with them. There were always some uproarious moments, but I never saw children get out of hand when he was in charge of them. And by the end of the afternoon, his chief work was to make them forget that they did really want their tea!

All this time a veritable army of women was in the adjoining hall getting the tea ready. The large hall was full of long tables, the white cloths almost hidden by the food – platefuls of sandwiches and biscuits, cakes and tarts and sponges, all made by the women of the church. They had soon got to know Doctor's taste for sweet things and there was always a plate of what they had learned were his favourites, kept aside for him. It was all warm-hearted and generous and there was always an open invitation for all to share in the tea, and the little Sunday School scholars knew that their 'mams' and often their dads too would be welcome at the tables whether they were members or not.

I remember one little incident very vividly.

When all the children were seated (they were always the first to get their tea), a worried member of the church came to Doctor and said, 'Doctor, there are half-a-dozen or so Catholic children at the tables, and it's not fair, they have their Whitsun treat tomorrow. Shall I send them out?' He was speaking to the wrong man! 'Oh no! don't do that, they're only children, let them stay,' said Doctor. Muttering that it wasn't fair, the poor man went away. But, as he walked from the chapel to the hall, he had a bright idea. He would be falling in with Doctor's wishes, but he went into the hall, called for silence, and said: 'Father M— is outside and I think he is looking for someone . . .' He had said enough – enough to send five or six shadowy little figures slinking hurriedly out of the hall! It was some days before the story reached Doctor's ears, and though he could not hide an unwilling smile at the clever ploy, yet I think his heart was a little sore for the children – he always had a very tender spot for them.

But, to return to our concert. It came to an end when a messenger from the hall whispered a word in Mr Rees's ear, and he made the announcement that tea was ready. He organized the transit from chapel to hall, and, whether you had been running races in the open air, or singing your heart out in a crowded chapel, there was nothing like a good cup of tea in good company. We all enjoyed ourselves thoroughly and went home happy with our hearts warmed to one another; thus the Whitsun treat was over for another year.

I spare you the story of the washing up and the clearing away, after a party of very nearly a thousand people.

We had no dishwashing machines, but with everybody anxious to help, the chore became yet another opportunity for fellowship.

5
SUMMER, 1932

I suppose that what Martyn and I did during holiday times hardly comes within the ambit of this account, but there was one summer holiday, during our time at Aberavon, so different from anything that we had ever known, that it must be mentioned.

In the ordinary way August was our holiday month and we spent it mostly with our families and friends, at first with Martyn's family in London or with mine in Harrow. Then the removal of the latter to Newcastle Emlyn took us there. The loan of the schoolmaster's house in Talybont, or of Professor Morris Jones' house in Aberystwyth widened our horizon and opened out some delightful discoveries of places ideal for rest and relaxation, *and* for interest for our fast-growing daughter. Some of these places and the things that sometimes happened in them are described in another place and I will not repeat myself. Martyn could be perfectly happy in most places so long as we always let him have the mornings to himself to read and study and think – holiday or not! But the summer of 1932 was completely different. Martyn had a letter from a certain Dr Richard Roberts, minister of Sherbourne Street Presbyterian church in Toronto. This man had been minister of the Welsh Church in Willesden Green, London and, though the two, with a generation between them, had never met, Dr Roberts had heard all about this young man, over the Welsh 'grape-vine'. With some trepidation, but reassured by the new man's evident sincerity and mental ability, and his undoubted popularity (for after all, he had now been in the ministry for some five years), Dr Roberts wrote to ask him to fill the Sherbourne Street pulpit for July and August 1932.

The sights were clear and the invitation was accepted, with the proviso that his wife and daughter would come with him! There was one hurdle to be cleared – the care and welfare of 'the Forward'. Without being happy about that, he felt he could not go. But there was what one can only regard as true providential provision at hand. There was an elderly retired minis-

ter living in Cardiff – the Rev. Wynn Thomas.
He had preached at Sandfields, and was a very
acceptable 'supply' preacher on some of Martyn's
'away' Sundays. Martyn asked him if he, with
Mrs Thomas, would come and live in our Manse,
and be the resident minister during our absence
in Canada. He consented to do this, and it was
a complete success. His consent set us packing
– Oh! our ignorance! – we took a trunk, a travelling trunk, and it was the greatest nuisance at
every turn. However, one learns.

The day came when we boarded the old
Olympic in Southampton and, as we sailed away,
we could see the figures of our two mothers,
Martyn's and mine, waving good-bye and getting smaller and smaller, till all we could see were
two coloured spots, one blue and one brown,
before they disappeared altogether – and I was
convinced I would never see them, or indeed, dry
land again! The dry land, it is true, we saw very
soon, because we called at Cherbourg before
heading for the open sea. Elizabeth, at four-and-
a-half, took it all in her stride and enjoyed all
the fun and games in the supervised nursery or
playroom. Martyn's life was exactly the same as
if we were at home. As for me, I couldn't really
enjoy it, because I was frightened and my imagination ran riot. I remember lying awake in my

bunk and thinking: There's only the thickness of the sides of the ship between me and the Atlantic and untold horrors!

Then came the fog, and the foghorns blaring out their warning every three minutes while it lasted, a mournful sound. One night in mid-Atlantic I remember well. It was pitch dark and the thick fog was really a wet drizzle. I was just going into the main lounge when one of the ship's officers began to speak to me. He looked pale and dreary, and, 'Rotten night,' said he. 'Yes, I don't like it,' I replied. He went on, 'It was a night just like this when the *Titanic* went down.' (Oh, help!) 'We were going along like this and then came the alarm and every ship within a reasonable distance of the spot had to go there at once and try to pick up survivors. We had to change course and we beat our own speed record. But we had been too far away, and were too late to help anyone.'

I could see that he was reliving the whole episode; he was depressed and miserable, and I was very thankful when he was called away. Martyn thought it was hilarious that this should have happened to *me*, and when I saw the funny side through his eyes, my equilibrium was soon restored. But after all these years I can remember the incident and the gloom very well.

It was during this voyage that Elizabeth learnt to read. There were long hours of time to fill, and a child can't play *all* the time. I had the idea that it might interest her and certainly solve, to some degree, the problem of boredom, and the 'What can I do now?' syndrome! Of course we had no suitable book from which she could learn, so I had to print sentences for her, and armed with phonetics and memory and a strong desire to enter into the mysteries, she ploughed on. I always remember the first sentence that we attacked: THE FAT CAT SAT ON THE MAT!!

The sails were set and she was off! She was 'reading', laboriously, by the time we reached New York, and has never stopped since.

We arrived in bright sunshine but in a very dispirited New York. The depression of the last few years was still upon the people. We were met by the parents of a friend of Vincent Lloyd-Jones. They had been very wealthy people, but were now reduced to what they regarded as poverty, as were so many at that time in New York. But they were gracious and kindly hosts to us for a day or two before putting us on the train to Toronto, always bemoaning the situation, and comparing what they were able to do for us with what they *might* have done a few months earlier.

We arrived in Toronto about mid-day after a

very uncomfortable over-night train journey. Dr Roberts and a few others met us and took us to '74 St George' – a beautiful old house, now a guest house, where we were to stay. That was on July 1, a Friday. I quite intended to keep a diary – and so I did, for exactly three days! July 1 gives the account of our arrival; July 2, a description of our temporary home and a note of the fact that Dr Roberts took Martyn out to introduce him to the various available libraries (first priority!) and, as an afterthought, the Bank! Apparently Toronto made an impression of sheer beauty on me. I say: 'It is a most lovely town – the residential part lovely with lawns like velvet and trees everywhere. Apparently when they make a new road they plant trees along it.'

My third and last entry is for Sunday, July 3rd, I give the entry in full:

> Morning service at 11.00. Martyn went early with assistant, we came with Miss Stevenson. Very beautiful church, elaborate decoration and carpeted. Gallery at back only. Dr Roberts took the service, Randall (assistant) read the lessons and Martyn preached – strange to see him in a gown [he did not wear a gown in Sandfields] but it did not trouble him. He preached: 'Unto you therefore which believe he is precious.' There

was a good congregation and they listened well. It was a very good service with moments of great tension. At the end many were appreciative, many testified that they felt they were not Christians at all. Many were grateful for 'this oasis in the desert'. Went to Dr Roberts' home for dinner and tea - much praise of sermon and assurances that Martyn was following up Dr Roberts' own theme. Evening service – pretty good congregation, greater number than usual but not quite full, service broadcast: 'Enter ye in at the strait gate.' People listened in dead silence – feel there was conviction – obviously not used to hearing the simple gospel message in that way – Mr Randall took us home in his car after a very informal reception in the vestry for us to meet the church members. (I met Laura Samuel who left Newcastle Emlyn 20 years ago!)

End of entry and end of diary-keeping too. That morning there was a distinguished-looking little old lady present. As she approached in the hand-shaking 'line' at the end of the service, Dr Roberts told Martyn that she was an enormously wealthy woman – owner of a series of huge stores ('the size of Selfridge's', said Dr Roberts) in every big town right across the country. As she shook hands with Martyn she said: 'Dr Lloyd-Jones, did

I understand you to say that for these two months you will be preaching chiefly to Christians in the mornings and chiefly to non-believers or doubtful Christians in the evenings?' 'Yes,' said Martyn, 'as a general guide-line, that is my custom.' 'Well,' said she firmly and earnestly, 'from now on I shall come in the evenings.' She was as good as her word and never missed a service; she had never been known to come to an evening service before.

Those two months in Sherbourne Street were remarkable. The congregation just grew and grew with every passing Sunday. For the last two or three it was packed, with chairs in the aisles and every available space, and people sitting on the pulpit stairs. Special police were sent to control the traffic, and at their request, the meetings were started early; as soon, that is, as there was no more room inside. Dr Roberts himself was not an evangelical, but never showed resentment. I think he was pleased that his choice of vacation supply had been successful. He had chosen not to go away for his vacation, quite an unheard-of decision, but rather to stay at home, especially as one of his daughters was to be married during the time we were there. But he prevailed upon Martyn to go to Chatauqua in his stead, for the inside of a week. And it was the story of Sherbourne

Street all over again: at the beginning, a complete unknown from the U.K., giving the morning lecture in a lesser hall, and finishing up at the end of the series with thousands crowding the great auditorium to hear this same unknown. Many interesting things happened during these two months in Toronto. Some have become vague memories, shrouded by the mists of time and age, but some still have the power – like Wordsworth's daffodils – to 'flash upon that inward eye, which is the bliss of solitude'. It was interesting to meet Dr T. T. Shields, often described as the 'Canadian Spurgeon', a good, evangelical preacher, but, according to many, spoiling his ministry by his unceasing diatribes against liberals and Roman Catholics.

One way and another we saw a great deal of the countryside and I found it very interesting. Travelling by train one day, I saw strip farming for the first time. The farms were not arranged like the hub of a wheel, with the farmlands clustered round them. On the contrary, the farmhouses were like a long row of detached houses in a fashionable quarter. The farm lands stretched away from the houses in parallel strips, their limit being some road or river. I was fascinated and remarked on this unusual arrangement, and was told that it was not at all uncommon, but very popular with the farmers, as they were all within a few hundred yards or so of their neighbours, and so did not get so lonely – a great boon to the early settlers. Another of their very bright and original ideas was to mark their boundaries with the roots of trees. Fencing was out of the question, for the settlers were very poor. The easiest thing was to use the roots of the trees uprooted to clear the land. We saw many of these 'hedges'. The great roots set on end and entangled with each other looked more like ramparts than fences, but they were very effective and they have lasted for a long, long time.

I was unlucky one day. Some new friends took us out, and as we went along the country roads, we noticed that the roadside was lined with raspberry bushes, which were full of fruit. It was hot and we were thirsty and the fruit looked inviting. We stopped and enjoyed quite a feast. What I did not realize was that, while I was eating the fruit, the mosquitoes were eating my ankles! I was laid up for three days with ankles like balloons and desperately itchy! As I said before – we learn!

We had one lovely trip a couple of hundred miles up North into the wilds and the lakes. Every now and then we would drive through a 'Village', very unlike those in the homeland. Just a kind of inn, a petrol pump and a few wooden 'shacks' or bungalow-type houses. *But* – in one of these little settlements, there was a central open space, with a strong post driven into the middle of it, and, tethered to the post, was a little brown bear! joy and delight for Elizabeth together with a delicious shiver of fear! But it was all right. All it wanted was a bottle of pop. The empties lay in dozens all around him on the ground, but he was still thirsty. We gave him one and he drank it greedily, holding the bottle upside down to drain the last drop, and then, to shrieks of delight from Elizabeth, held it to his eye to see if there might be just one drop left! We thought we would have to leave Elizabeth there with him, but when we promised we would see him again on our return journey, she grudgingly submitted to being driven away.

Actually our stay at the lake-side ranch-type hotel was delightful, though we were very, very grateful for the nets to keep the mosquitoes away at night. I was roused from a deep sleep of sheer exhaustion and fresh air, to hear loud voices just below our window, and the crunch of wheels on gravel and the snorting and pawing of horses. 'Red Indians' I decided, my heart pounding, and I was just about to wake Martyn up, when I found myself fully awake and recognizing the arrival of late visitors! Unlikely? Very, but perfectly true!

I had quite a lesson one day during a train journey (from where to where I cannot remember) but I was enjoying every minute of it, letting my eyes rest on the beauties of hilly, wooded country. We were running along one side of a valley. Across the wide valley, on the other side was rising land, covered with trees – dark green conifers, their pointed tops reaching towards the sun. Then I noticed that, right in the middle of the front row of trees, was a different tree. It was a glowing, gold red colour and looked so very beautiful against the dark background. We were getting out at the next stop which we were fast approaching, and I asked one of the men who met us the name of the tree. 'Isn't it beautiful?' said I. 'Yes,' he said, 'it does look good there, but it is quite dead, you know. It will stay like that for the summer, but it will be broken to bits by the ice and snow and gales when the hard weather comes – there's no life in it.' I *had* to believe him. I could see it all. And I thought to myself - that is just like ourselves! We may appear to be wonderful Christians, but it is the 'hard weather' which will test us to see if we have life in us.

I suppose that the highlight of our actual sightseeing was the day we went to Niagara. There was a family living in Toronto who were closely related to friends of ours in Llanelli, South Wales. We had made some contact with them and been to their home already. Elizabeth was delighted that Marian, aged twelve, was willing to play with her. To the sorrow of their relatives, they were not overly interested in spiritual matters, but we found them kind and very anxious that we should see all the wonders possible in the time we had at our disposal. They arranged the trip to Niagara and we had a never-to-be-forgotten day. It was a breath-taking experience to stand within a few yards of the great St Lawrence River emptying itself over the cliff in clouds of spray, to continue its journey.

But there was more to see – over the bridge to the American side, and down, through what seemed like solid rock, in a lift which let us out at the foot of the falls. It had been a terrific view from the top, but from here it was almost too much! And we mused over and marvelled at the fact of all that tremendous power, harnessed by man to provide a great area of the land with all its needed electricity! The God who created Niagara has surely created great brain power and ability in man. We finished that visit with lunch in the Seagram tower – rather like the Post Office tower in London – and had a glorious panoramic view of the whole area. Strangely enough, when

Elizabeth re-visited Niagara a few years ago with her own family, she remembered nothing of her visit when four-and-a-half years old, until she stood again at the foot of the falls.

In the very nature of things it was apparent that Martyn would be making some peregrinations without us. Such, for instance, was his visit to Chatauqua, and there were several other such calls. But Dr Roberts remembered that he was on holiday, and he persuaded Martyn to go with him on a fishing trip to the lakes. They went, from a Monday to a Friday. Martyn had never in his life done anything like that before – and he never did it again. It was really wild country with a series of lakes, like beads strung together, surrounded by hills and trees and thick vegetation that had never known the restraining hand of man. Dr Roberts knew of certain primitive lodging places, so that they need not sleep under canvas. Mosquitoes and a peculiarly nasty kind of smaller flying insects, which were a constant cause of irritation and annoyance, were the only wild-life they encountered. The fishing was done from a type of rowing boat, and they were accompanied by an Indian who rowed the boat, and dragged it along dry land from one lake to the next. The hunted prey were lake trout, and Martyn, for the only time in his life, caught a number of fish, including one enormous creature as big as a fair-sized salmon, all by himself. He insisted on being photographed with it, in case no one would believe his story! We ate it that weekend, and it was delicious. The whole week had done him a world of good and he came home looking like a Red Indian.

One of Elizabeth's memories is of a very 'grand' dinner which she attended with us. Mrs Fudger, the wealthy old lady, had invited us, and when she understood that to leave Elizabeth with total strangers was difficult, indeed made acceptance impossible, she insisted that we bring her too. So, while we and the Roberts family and a few others sat at the great dining table, Elizabeth had a tiny table all to herself a few yards from where I was sitting, where she and her dolly were waited on hand and foot.

But – and this is what chiefly interests me as I look back – an incident occurred as we were about to leave. We had said our farewells and were just getting into the car when there was a wail of misery – dolly was left behind! Martyn turned and went back up the steps to the front door – it was like a sheet of solid steel! He found a bell and rang it, we could hear it in the distance. In a minute or two a small panel was pushed back and a grating, about 6 inches square, appeared, and an anxious face peered out at us, then another and yet another. We explained our plight, there was a conference, then a kind of order was given, and, at length a small door in the 'iron curtain' was opened just wide enough for an arm holding the doll to come through. We took the doll, the arm was withdrawn, and the door was shut at speed. Nobody waited for our thanks, they had had a real fright, and did not feel safe till the steel door was all shut up again. In 1932 it seemed incredible, and really rather silly, but not today!

At length came the last Sunday in August, the packed meetings, and the warm farewells. We were to sail from Quebec, which meant a long train journey and a night in Quebec.

All our Toronto friends said: 'You *must* stay at the *Château Frontenac*, a great hotel topping a towering cliff above Quebec – the last word in luxury hotels!

We arrived in Quebec with no idea how to proceed to our 'Château', or anywhere else. All was confusion, and as French as France. Then suddenly I saw a little 'office', just a large desk with a lady sitting at it, and a notice above to the effect that English was spoken there! Oasis in the desert! We went over and asked how we could get to the *Château Frontenac*, as we had to wait till next day for the boat. And this very nice person looked at us for a minute, her eyes softening as they rested on Elizabeth, and she said: 'Why do you want to go to the *Château*?' Martyn said that we had been advised – or rather pressed – to do so, and we did not know where else to go. She made up her mind: 'You do not want to go there. You do not want to take that little one there. She would be much happier in the Y.W.C.A., it is a very pleasant place at which to stay. I will order a cab for you.'

We hardly knew that we were being managed, but we found ourselves in the Y.W.C.A., and agreed that she was quite right! It was a most beautiful old house surrounded by lawns, reminiscent of 74 St George, but on a bigger scale. We luxuriated in the coolness and the comfort and the quiet, and saw a little of Quebec before boarding *The Empress of Britain* the next day, and sailing without incident, after a never-to-be-forgotten experience.

The whole time we were away, Martyn wrote a weekly letter to the church at Sandfields. Each letter could well be called the diary of the week – an account of all that he did, his remarks on the services, and some of the responses he got from his hearers; all the thoughts evoked in him by what he saw and heard; in fact a running commentary on the week – and always the expression of his concern for the well-being of his flock at Sandfields. In fact they were truly pastoral letters. Mr Wynn Thomas would read them to the Church, and Martyn was very happy to think that in them was a full and comprehensive account of his eight weeks in Canada. But, alas! no one has ever seen those letters since, and no one knows what happened to them. I suppose that Mr Thomas never thought about giving them to Mr E. T. Rees for the church archives, and that Mr Rees did not like to ask for them. Nobody knows. When Mr Wynn Thomas died (his wife had pre-deceased him) we did write to the people responsible for clearing up his affairs and possessions. We asked them to save the letters for us if they ever came across them. But they never arrived. Had they done so, this chapter might well have become a book. I am sure it would have been rich and enjoyable reading.

Martyn crossed the Atlantic again in 1937, but without his family, for Ann had joined us in the January of that year and was barely six months old. She and Elizabeth and I stayed with my parents in Harrow while Martyn preached in the United States. I have a veritable library of letters which would probably tell the whole story of his visit, but they would all have to be translated from the Welsh. Perhaps they will find themselves in print at a later date. There is no doubt that Martyn had a very fruitful and interesting six weeks and met many precious, kindred souls. But in every letter is the complaint of homesickness – sometimes less, sometimes more – and the declaration that he would never again take a trip like that on his own – and he never did!

*1. Bethlehem Forward Movement Church,
popularly known as 'Sandfields'.*

*2. With Martyn and Elizabeth on holiday in Cwmyreglwys,
Pembrokeshire, 1933.*

3. With Elizabeth.

4. Elizabeth at Llanelly.

5. The Brotherhood on a visit to Llangeitho.

6. The Young Women's Sunday School Class, Sandfields.

7. 'The Compleat Angler'.

8. The three of us with the Wanglands at Niagara Falls.

9. The little bear asking for more!

10. Martyn in lakeland on the fishing trip.

11. *Sherbourne Street Church, Toronto.*

12. *With Martyn and Elizabeth in Canada.*

6

WILLIAM NOBES

I cannot remember the time when William Nobes first came among us, nor can I remember a time when he was not there. We did not think of him as old, though he was retired from his work. Known affectionately to his friends as Nobby, his older nick-name from his working days would sometimes crop up. It puzzled me – 'Why Kingy?', I asked one who had just used the name. 'Oh well, he used to be a navvy, you see', was the answer I got, which was meant to explain everything. For some unknown reason every navvy was a 'Kingy'.

William Nobes, a lean, almost boyish, figure, was always meticulously clean and neat and had a beautiful face: regular features and clear blue eyes, clean-shaven with a pink and white complexion and white hair, and always a pleasant expression with a ready smile. He was quiet and unobtrusive and not given to public utterance. Only once do I remember hearing him speak and that was truly an occasion to be remembered. It was at the Fellowship Meeting.

The talk had been free and often moving, when something said, or some inner constraint, brought William Nobes to his feet, and he told us the story of his conversion. He did not speak glibly or even easily, but hesitantly. He was soft-voiced with a 'burr' that spoke of one of the Southern counties. Every eye was fixed upon him and we waited for what he had to say with something more than an expectant hush.

He said little about his early days, or whether he had Christian forbears. I do not know whether he had experienced previous pangs of conscience or agonies of conviction - how I wish I had asked him more at the time! My impression is that he had never been a violent, aggressive sinner, but he was completely indifferent to God and had not the faintest interest in spiritual things. And then, with his youth behind him, when he was well on to middle age, he had a dream.

The horror of that dream was real to him yet, and he managed, in the hush of that meeting, to involve us, too, in the horror of it. In his dream he was hanging over a flaming inferno, helpless and frantic. Above him and almost obstructing the opening of the pit was an enormous ball, like a great globe, and he found himself trying to climb up the roundness of this ball to get away from the heat of the flames below, and out into the clean, cool air above. Sometimes he would make two or three feet, sometimes more, at times only two or three inches.

Once he thought he had really got over the widest part of the ball, but in spite of all his efforts and his mounting fear and agony, the result was always the same – he would fail to keep his hold, fail to make another inch, fail to keep what ground he had gained, and in helpless weakness slide and slither back along that fearsome slope, to find himself back where he had started.

This seemed to go on for an eternity, and then at last, all hope gone, and hanging over the open jaws of hell, he looked up once more at the light above him and uttered one great despairing cry – and there was a face in that light looking down at him, full of love and pity, and a hand reached down and grasped his, and drew him up out of all the horror below him and stood him on the firm sweet earth and in the pure clear air.

What did David say? ' . . . he inclined unto me, and heard my cry. He brought me up also out of an horrible pit . . . and set my feet upon a rock, and established my goings. And he hath put a new song in my mouth, even praise unto our God' (*Psa.* 40:1–3). All these words William Nobes could say too, and they were all true of him. From then on he walked before the Lord in love and thankfulness.

William Nobes was very poor in this world's goods. The meagre pension of the time kept body and soul together, and paid the rent of his little bachelor room. But no one ever heard him grumble or complain. 'There's just four of us now', was his contented answer to someone who asked him about family and relatives, 'my bed and my table, my Book and me'!

Someone might feel that, although his name is written in heaven, there is not much to write about his earthly life. Perhaps not, but apart from the sweetness of his nature William Nobes had one rare and precious gift, a surprising gift, one might think, in one of so shy and retiring a nature. He could talk about God and spiritual things to anybody and everybody at any time and in any place, *without offence.*

There was a window-sill in the open place outside the entrance to the market. It caught all the available sunshine and William Nobes could usually be found sitting there, chatting happily in his gentle, kindly manner to any and all who had time to stop and talk to him.

When sometimes we came across the havoc wrought by the blundering unwisdom of some of the most well-meaning Christians, we knew that the gift of this unobtrusive gentle disciple of the Lord, was of a very high order indeed, and always felt that he must have his place, if not among the three 'mighties', then surely among the thirty!

William Nobes died as he had lived, quietly and peacefully. He had no family, no living relations of any kind as far as anyone knew, but he was the son of the King, and on the day of his funeral there was no lack of 'family' to lay his earthly frame to rest, 'in sure and certain hope of the resurrection'. Even on this, his last journey, William Nobes was still bearing his witness – the sight of the large company of his fellow church members – his family – following the Minister behind the simple coffin, wending their way through the town, and up the long three miles to the cemetery on the mountain side, spoke to the hearts of many – curious, interested, careless, thoughtful – onlookers. It reminded them again, in the midst of the busy-ness of everyday life, of those 'unseen things' which the Word of God tells us 'are eternal'.

7

MARK McCANN

One Sunday night, I was early in my seat at the back of the church, and as Johnnie Mort entered and was about to proceed to his usual place at the front, he hesitated, then stopped and whispered to me, 'I've got one of the Devil's Generals here tonight, Mrs Jones, pray for him to be converted.'

I looked with interest at the man following him down the aisle, and as the service proceeded, found it difficult not to listen with *his* ears to all that was said. The service came to an end and many members of the congregation left during the retiring hymn, before the after-meeting. Among them were Johnnie Mort and his friend.

As they came up the aisle I was able to have a more satisfactory look at the visitor. I saw a thin, tallish, raw-boned man, thin grey hair well plastered down, a slightly embarrassed expression and an incredible moustache! It was carefully waxed, to stick straight out on each side, and – measured from tip to tip – was a good deal wider than his long thin face. It was his pride and joy and he would fight to defend its title to be the longest moustache, as fiercely as any knight of old might have defended the honour of his lady-love.

In the course of the next few days, Johnnie Mort came to report to us and to tell us a little of the man's story. His name was Mark McCann, a Scot on his father's side, Irish on his mother's. He was probably in his early sixties and was at one time a miner. But work, it seems, had always been a secondary interest in his life. His time was chiefly taken up in going from one fair to the next, sometimes travelling many miles, walking and thumbing lifts to this end – and the purpose of it all? – fights! They were the very breath of life to him. He said himself that he would go anywhere for a good fight.

His cronies knew exactly how to rouse him. A few drinks and then almost any pin-prick of a challenge or an insult would do. The infallible fury-rouser was any aspersion cast on his moustache – that so and so had a better one or a longer one. Then the fight was on.

There was no doubt about his prowess in this field, he was a tremendous fighter. His unusually long arms gave him the advantage of a long reach, the walking kept him fit, and he had plenty of exercise. But above and beyond all he had an uncontrollable temper – once in the grip of it he was virtually insane. To knock out his adversary was not enough. According to himself in one of his rare moments of self-revelation, he must kill, and to this end he would leap on the prostrate, defeated man and shake him and bang his head against the ground, with no more thought of desisting than a vicious dog savaging his victim.

This propensity had frightened him, and as he himself recognized the fact that he was getting worse instead of better, he always made sure before starting a fight that he had two cronies with him, to hold him back from further attack once he had knocked out his man. These would help him to cool down and then collect the victor's purse!

Mark McCann once gave me another terrible illustration of this insane temper. He had come in for his dinner one day and his well-filled plate was on the table. He stopped to wash his hands in the outer kitchen and when he got to the table he found the dog eating his dinner! He told me – with bowed head and averted eyes – that he took that dog out to the kitchen sink and cut its head off with a bread knife! These things were not told in any spirit of bravado or inverted self-glory, but with deep shame, muttered in a low voice as though he must tell the worst and be reassured again of the everlasting mercy.

That first Sunday night Mark McCann was arrested by the Spirit of God. He did not know enough to stay to the after-meeting and Johnnie Mort wisely said nothing to him, though he could see that a work was being done. On the following Sunday we had a visiting minister.

Somewhat to Johnnie Mort's surprise, at the end of the evening service, McCann whispered his intention of staying to the after-meeting, which he did, Johnnie Mort at his side, wondering and half unbelieving. He stood in response to the invitation, was received with a solemn joy and from that moment showed himself to be a changed man, unfailingly faithful, truly born again – another, somewhat elderly, 'babe' for the church to love and nurture.

Many months later he told me that he knew in his heart he had been converted that first night, but had been too shy, or too nervous, or too . . . – he knew not what – to declare it. All that week an inner anxiety grew in him, that he had missed his opportunity, that God might have given him up. Never had a week gone so slowly, but as his anxiety mounted so did his determination, and when on the second Sunday evening in the after-meeting, the invitation came, it was like a life-line to a drowning man. 'I was sorry it wasn't the Doctor there,' he said, 'I would have liked to wait for him to receive me, but I didn't dare wait another week!'

Mark McCann had a family, a wife and four or five grown children, the youngest a girl of about fifteen. The only one who had any apparent gleam of intelligence was the eldest son, Tom, who, unfortunately, delighted in using what he had to stumble his father. I never ceased to be amazed at the way the Lord helped his father with an answer when hard-pressed, or with a word in season when it was wanted, for he knew absolutely nothing of spiritual things at first. I remember well an example of this which he told me in his own half-hesitant, half-apologetic way – anxious to know if what he had said was right:

Son: Dad, you say Jesus Christ was very good, don't you?

McCann: Oh yes, son, oh yes. He was good, very good, the very, very best.

Son: Well, you believe war and fighting are bad things, don't you?

McCann: Oh yes, son, yes, very bad, oh
  very bad.

Son: Well, it says in the Bible that Jesus
  Christ told his disciples they were to
  get swords!

What should he say? He did not know that the
Lord had promised 'a mouth and wisdom, which
all your adversaries shall not be able to gainsay
nor resist' (*Luke* 21:15), but he was to prove it
then and at many other times. The end of the
conversation came as McCann said: 'Well, son,
well, if the Bible says that Jesus Christ told us
to take a sword, it must be to cut our sins off of
us!'

Not what you would find in a commentary or
a theological treatise, but sufficient for the purpose and very effective! Tom had turned on his
heel and gone, without another word.

The members of his family never showed any
interest in the state of their souls, but while Mark
McCann lived they all had to attend the Sunday
services. Whether they were afraid of him and
the rages that had terrified them for so long,
or whether they were grateful to an 'unknown
God', associated with the Chapel, for the peace
they now enjoyed, I do not know; but while he
lived they all trooped obediently in with him to
the Sunday services. As for him he rejoiced and

revelled in it all and seemed to have a true spiritual understanding, a God-given instinct for what was right, although completely ignorant and untaught from a human point of view.

One Wednesday night at the Church Fellowship meeting, some few weeks after his conversion, Mark McCann was, as usual, in his seat towards the back of the hall, enjoying every word of the discussion, drinking everything in, but never speaking. I cannot remember that he ever said a word in public. At the end of the meeting, after the benediction, Doctor took up his customary position at the door to exchange a word and a handshake with the departing members, and among them came McCann – but now a hardly recognizable McCann – the moustache, his pride and joy, was gone, and all that was left was a small, neatly-trimmed, ordinary and unobtrusive substitute on his upper lip!

Recovering from the surprise, and with various explanations for the phenomenon surging through his mind, Doctor said: 'Mr McCann, will you wait for a few minutes? I would like just a word with you.' He was afraid that some insensitive, if well-meaning, busybody had been 'getting at' this new convert, and he asked who had told him to cut off his moustache? 'Nobody, Doctor, nobody told me to do it.' 'Well then, why did you do it?' Again, the embarrassed shuffle, the hesitation and near stammer – 'Well, Doctor, it was one morning when I was shaving, and I looked at myself in the mirror, and I looked at my moustache, and I said to myself – them things isn't for Christians, and I cut it off!' He was wholehearted from the beginning. As he learned of other things which 'isn't for Christians', they had to go. Drink was never a problem, but his temper was, and his recognition of this, and his success in dealing with it, were little short of heroic.

One evening, as we were leaving the hall at the end of a weeknight meeting. I passed a small group of three or four people talking to McCann. As I said 'Good-night' and went by, one of the group said: 'Isn't it a shame, Mrs Jones, Mr Mc-Cann can't read.' 'Can't read?' – I was quite surprised. 'No' – 'There's a pity' – 'He never learnt, see' – 'He'd love to be able to read' – 'He can't read his Bible'.

A veritable chorus of murmurs and comments broke out, McCann meanwhile shuffling his feet and hanging his head.

'Can't you read at all, Mr McCann?' I asked. 'No, I never learnt, I never went to school regular, see, I was always running away, so I can't read.'

Despair and hopelessness all round! Well, I knew it was easy enough to teach a child to read, and even as the thought came to my mind that it might be more difficult with a man in his middle or late fifties, it was immediately snuffed out by a mental picture of my mother teaching old Mr Matthews – well on in his seventies – to read, and she never seemed to have any difficulty.

I must digress for a moment here, for this Mr Matthews deserves honourable mention. He was a farmer all his life, in the Vale of Glamorgan, starting as a farm hand in a tied cottage. Like many of his contemporaries in the same walk of life he had never been to school, and from a child knew nothing but hard work. He had grown up and married and brought up a large family of children on the princely sum of 9 shillings a week!

He had been gloriously converted in the 1904–5 revival, when, I think, he was nearer seventy than sixty. He had seen and felt the Holy Spirit working in great power and the wonder and the glory of that revival never left him. But he could not read and was conscious of a great deprivation in not being able to study the Bible. Now he had come to live, in retirement, with his married daughter in Harrow. She was a sincere Christian, as was her husband. They had three beautiful children and the family attended an English church. Mr Matthews had no English and he was a member of the Welsh church which we as a family attended.

One day my mother told us that Mr Matthews was going to learn to read, and would be coming every morning for lessons. We were greatly intrigued. Perhaps we found it hard to believe that anyone should *want* to have lessons! However the pupil came and, after all these years, I can see them now in my mind's eye.

In our old-fashioned house we had what we knew as 'the drawing room'. It opened into a glass house which we grandly called 'the Conservatory' and in one or other of these rooms they would sit. As our baby brother would say, 'When it's fine they sit in the "d'awin' moon" and if it's wet, in the "scuvetry"!' Of course, the large-print Bible, opened out on the table between them, was a Welsh one and Welsh is a phonetic language. In no time at all Mr Matthews was reading, slowly and haltingly at first with a finger picking out the words, but soon with ease and great delight. When he first picked out the word *Iesu* (Jesus) he broke down completely, and with the tears running down his cheeks, and crying, 'Oh, his name, his blessed name!', he picked up the book and kissed that name.

I am sure that it was the memory of this that helped to dispel, in a split-second, the doubt in my mind concerning the possibility of teaching an elderly man to read. Be that as it may, I said, with the complete confidence of comparative youth and inexperience, 'I'm sure I can teach you to read, Mr McCann, if you would like to try.' Pity help me! I little knew what I was taking on! McCann was delighted and jumped at the offer and we arranged the times for the sessions.

The first few minutes of the first session told me all! I had picked out one of our daughter Elizabeth's reading-books. It was a small book with a picture on one page and a few simple words on the facing page; it was called *The Little Red Hen!* We got nowhere. Phonetics? We might as well have tried Chinese characters. Inwardly I was in despair and grieving over what I knew would be a bitter blow for him.

We ploughed on, with no hope at all on my part, for two or three sessions. Then – it must have been the third or fourth time he came – as I got out the book and put it before him on the table, he pushed it away. Half apologetically and half rebelliously, he said: 'I don't want to read that, I want to read the Bible.' I confess I felt rebuked! 'Right', I said, 'let's do that', and I fetched a clear-print Bible and opened it at the

Gospel of John, Chapter 10, verse 11: 'I am the good shepherd . . .' With his finger pushing along under each word, he started, spelling each word aloud, getting an occasional little word by himself, looking for prompting over the big ones: 'I' . . . 'a,m', then very hesitantly 'am', 't,h,e'??? Seeing him flounder, I said, 'It doesn't sound like anything, does it? You must just remember that t,h,e always spells 'the'. Complete satisfaction! He never forgot, and now the door was wide open and the light began to dawn.

The method with Mark McCann was memory and the sound of the words, perhaps some familiarity with some of the sentences, but above and beyond all a sense of the preciousness of the words and an overpowering desire to read them. There was one more hitch. It became obvious that he must have reading-glasses. A sympathetic optician in the town provided them (and refused to let him pay for them), and once more we were well away. He would come for his lesson, sit at the table, produce the glasses and rub them lovingly with his handkerchief, invariably saying in his jerky, hesitant way, 'Lovely pebble in them glasses', and put them on with such pride!

After a time I began to wonder whether the definitely perceptible improvement in the reading might have been due to his retentive memory

– was he unconsciously memorizing John 10?! We turned to a chapter in Mark's Gospel – no progress! Even the travelling finger below the words produced no results, and so with one or two other passages. I confess to feeling a slight sinking sensation, but went back to John 10 every time, just to keep him happy.

Then one day it struck me that we might try John 1. We found the place, and, the finger at the ready, we started. It was remarkable. He worked his way along the line, very slowly and haltingly, with the occasional look for help, yet with a strange kind of confidence. At the end of the first verse, he stopped and looked at me over his glasses and said, 'Funny, isn't it? I can read John, but I can't read Mark, though it's me own name!'

After that I gave in, and we spent the reading hours in John's Gospel. I remember especially chapters 14 and 15. His joy knew no bounds and transformed his idle days. But it was not to last long.

One day, Mrs McCann came to the door to say that her husband was not well and could not come for his lesson, but would like to see me. I had not been too well myself but, as Doctor was away, I said I would go. I still remember the walk to his house, something less than a mile away.

It was a hot, end-of-June or early-July day, with the sun beating down mercilessly. However, that was as nothing to what I found in the house. I was taken into the small sitting-room and it was like walking into an oven.

The open fire-place held a blazing fire which roared its way up the chimney. Stretched between the door and the fire-place, almost blocking my entry, was a long, high table, and along it lay *something* covered with a sheet. For one moment I thought . . . but no! A movement to the right of the fire caught my eye, and there was Mark Mc Cann, chalk-white in face and propped up in his narrow bed, to enable him to breathe. He was obviously a very sick man.

He had always had what he called 'a weak chest', but this was no ordinary 'chestiness'. The pallor and the beads of sweat on head and face, the high fever and the frequent bouts of uncontrollable *rigor,* and the obvious degree of illness, all told their tale. The dreaded 'rubber lung', the result of youthful years spent working in the anthracite mines, had caught up with him, and Mark McCann was a dying man. His Bible and his glasses lay beside him on the bed, always within reach. The blazing fire was now explained. His wife and the family thought that the bouts of *rigor* meant that he was cold!

But what was under that white sheet? As, at last I rose to go, Mrs McCann, bursting with pride, said, 'Look, Mrs Jones', and drew back the sheet. And there – killed that morning and now lying in state – was a huge black sow! 'I'll send some bacon up to the Manse when we cut her up, Mrs Jones'. Near panic set in. 'Oh, no, don't do that. It would be a great pity to waste it.' 'What! not like a bit of bacon, Mrs Jones?' 'Well' (what could I say?), 'we shall be going away for a few weeks now, you see.' Explanation accepted!

We saw him several times after that before leaving for the Summer vacation. He was gentle and courteous, and was usually found, following with eyes and lips the finger that guided him still through the writings of his beloved John. The men from the church were very faithful in visiting him. They would arrange to go, three or four at a time, and pray with him and talk to him about the riches of his so-recently-found faith. For this he was grateful and full of peace and deep joy.

He seemed just to fade away, getting gradually weaker, until one day the Lord in his mercy took him out of all his suffering, to his home in Heaven, and the church rejoiced to know that another of our 'elderly babes' was safe for ever.

8

'STAFFORDSHIRE BILL'

'Staffordshire Bill' sat drinking in the Working Men's Club. He was a shapeless mass of a man, not very tall, but fat, and always appeared to be wearing several jerseys, cardigans, and coat upon coat, all at the same time. He had a heavy reddish face and a lugubrious expression. At close quarters it could be seen that the skin of his face was covered with innumerable tiny scars – the fruits of drunken orgies and the inevitable fights that followed in the fairs that he would never miss. It was his behaviour at fairs and his constant appeal for 'Fair play now, boys, fair play!' that earned him the other nickname by which he was known to all his fairground acquaintances – Billy Fairplay.

He was alone in the Club this Sunday afternoon but there was nothing strange in that. He was always alone. He had no friends and his fellow members in the Club invariably avoided sitting at his table. Many of them, it is true, were not paragons of virtue themselves, neither were they all as careful of their language as they might be. But Staffordshire Bill's filthy language and general unpleasantness were more than any of them could take, and to pass the time of day was as much as even the kindest of them could bring themselves to do.

Bill had a tiny long-suffering sparrow of a wife, and what kind of a life she lived, and what she endured, God alone knew. She never complained, and as she rarely went out and no one ever visited that house, very little was known of the home conditions. There was no evidence that he had ever used physical violence towards her. It would rather seem that he was always sodden in drink, morose and bad-tempered.

This was his third wife; how long they had been married I do not know. I remember meeting him in the street some months after his conversion, and making enquiries about her health. With tears on his cheeks and his voice trembling with emotion, he said he thanked God she was well and went on, 'She's a good woman, Mrs Jones, she's a good woman, and I thank God that for one that's been unlucky to lose them, I've been lucky to have a good one instead every time!' She outlived him, but as their village was some three or four miles up the valley from our church, she was not able to join us. She ended her days quietly in her own village among friendly neighbours.

William Thomas himself was nearly seventy when we first knew him, but he thought nothing of those three or four steep uphill miles when once 'the light of the knowledge of the glory of God in the face of Jesus Christ' had shined in his heart. He was at every meeting, twice on Sunday, Monday-night prayer-meeting, Wednesday-night Church Fellowship and Saturday-night Brotherhood, his old battered face transformed and radiant with an inner joy.

A deacon from one of the other churches in the town lived on his homeward route. His wife – the deacon's wife – told me that though she had been aware of him for many years, her usual view of him was almost incredible. I never knew what his work had been through the years, but latterly he had carried on a kind of door-to-door fish business, and for this purpose he had a small open cart – a kind of shallow wooden box with a plank of wood fixed from side to side to sit on, while the fish occupied the floor of the vehicle beneath him. He sat on this narrow seat, and as he was always drunk going home and as the road home was very steep, he invariably fell backwards off the seat, pillowed by the unsold fish, with his feet and legs sticking straight up in the air while his faithful little pony took him home to the ministrations of his long-suffering wife. That is how my friend, the deacon's wife had always seen him, until . . . but now I must go on with my story.

There he was, in the Club on a Sunday afternoon, drinking himself into his usual sodden condition, and as he afterwards confessed, feeling low, hopeless and depressed, trusting to the drink to drown those inward pangs and fears which sometimes disturbed him. There were several men in little groups of twos and threes in the Club room, drinking and talking, and suddenly he found himself listening, at first involuntarily, but then anxiously, to a conversation between two men at the table next to his.

'Staffordshire Bill' caught the words 'the Forward' and then something about the 'preacher', and then a complete sentence that was to change the whole of his life. 'Yes', said one man to the other, 'I was there last Sunday night and that preacher said nobody was hopeless – he said there was hope for everybody.' Of the rest of the conversation he heard nothing, but, arrested and now completely sobered, he said to himself, 'If there's hope for everybody, there's hope for me – I'll go to that chapel myself and see what that man says.'

Bill pulled out his old silver watch and saw that it was just about time for the evening service. He got up and, with the small gleam of hope driving him on against a heart full of trepidation, he walked the few hundred yards to the open gate of the railings that fenced the church, and stood there for two or three minutes. Then he lost his nerve, turned on his heel and went home!

What he suffered in that following week can only be left to the imagination. All we know is that the following Sunday evening saw him setting out, propelled by all the convicting power of the Holy Spirit, for 'the Forward'. As he came within earshot of the building he heard singing, and, arriving once more at the gate, realized that he was late, the service had started. With his heart in his boots and full of some nameless fear, he once more turned away and went home.

There was another week of misery, sometimes of despair, but there was no thought of turning back to the old ways, or any attempt to drown the terrible pangs of conscience or the terrors of conviction in drink.

In spite of all his sufferings nothing could snuff out altogether that little gleam lit in his heart by the words overheard two weeks before in the Working Men's Club. After all, God had begun a work in his heart, and 'the work which His goodness began, the arm of His strength will complete'. But William Thomas did not know that then.

The third Sunday dawned and found him once more wending his way to the chapel. Again, we can only guess at the state of his feelings and his thoughts. But now he had arrived at the gate, the people were going in, and he stood there wondering nervously what he should do next, when suddenly he felt a hand on his shoulder and the familiar cheerful voice of Johnnie Mort greeting him like a long-lost brother, and hiding his incredulous amazement in a very creditable way. His joy he did not try to hide. 'Are you coming in, Bill?', said he. 'Come and sit with me.'

That Sunday night 'Staffordshire Bill' was converted. There was no doubt about it: he was 'born again', he was 'translated from the kingdom of darkness into the kingdom of God's dear Son. Old things had passed away, all things had become new.' He found that he could understand the things that were being said, he believed the gospel and his heart was flooded with a great peace. The transformation in his face was remarkable; it now had the radiance of a saint.

At the end of the service there was always what we knew as the 'after-meeting'. It was held to give the opportunity to those who wished to come into the full membership and fellowship of the church to indicate that desire. There was no pressure made, but that night when the invitation was given, a trembling hand went up from Staffordshire Bill's corner and a murmur of joy and delight from all the rest of us. The Doctor said, 'Stand up, Mr Thomas, and let them see the latest monument to the grace of God'; and he stood and joined us, a very 'elderly babe' in Christ, but as precious to all the church as any new baby in a natural family.

As he walked out that night, lovingly attended by Johnnie Mort, they passed me, and Johnnie Mort said, 'Mrs Jones, this is Staffordshire Bill.' I shall never forget the agonized look on his face, as he flinched as though he had been struck a sudden blow. 'Oh no, Oh no,' he said, 'that's a bad old name for a bad old man; I am William Thomas now.' And that was typical of the man.

We had seen many evil livers become 'new men in Christ'. Some perhaps would be so amazed at the change in themselves, and the difference in themselves now from what they had once been, that they would tend to be too fond of talking about what sinners they had been, even sometimes to the extent of vying with each other as to who had been the greatest sinner! There was none of this in William Thomas; he was so deeply ashamed of his past that he could not bear to think about it, much less talk about it. Indeed, I often felt that his very joy was tinged with sorrow for the wasted years; but now the new life was before him and he was at peace and content. This battle was over, and the victory won.

What now? Now must follow that most necessary part of warfare – the 'follow-up operations', or clearing-up of pockets of resistance, and a constant vigilance. These operations could be numerous, and varied much in their form and in the strength of the resistance offered. Sometimes their very intransigence could make the poor warrior, if not his friends, wonder whether that first battle had really ended in victory or not. A lifetime of bad habits, the need of teaching and of understanding in spiritual matters, the lack of sympathy from family, friends and workmates, varying from a bored lack of interest to a vicious disapproval, and always the active attempts of the devil, using any and every opportunity and circumstance to hinder the growth of this new life – all such things show tough resistance to being dealt with.

William Thomas seemed to have little trouble with the lesser things, nor with some of the bigger hindrances either. His drinking habit just left him, with no effort on his part to deal with it. It had been a part of the whole of his adult life. There were not many days without drink playing a big part in them – not many evenings and nights when he was not totally incapacitated through alcohol. And yet, at his conversion, his desire for it left him and it was never a problem in his Christian life.

There were, however, other areas of fierce struggle, and heading the dark list was bad language. 'Staffordshire Bill' was foul-mouthed – so much so that even the toughest of his worldly acquaintances were sickened by him – one of the reasons why he always found himself left to his own company, in some deserted corner of the place where they were drinking. With his conversion came the conviction that he must do something about this. He realized that it was dishonouring to God and offensive to man. He must stop swearing and using bad language. But now he discovered that he was up against something that was too strong for him. He could not speak without swearing, he could not utter a sentence that was not peppered with oaths and blasphemies. He could not help it and he could not stop it.

The truth is that he did not know that he was doing it until the words were out, and then the realization that these horrible terms and words came from his own lips sickened and shamed him and he was driven to a frenzy of despair and to abject misery. It may seem strange that he never sought the help of a fellow Christian in this matter, but he was too ashamed, and he suffered for some weeks, little dreaming that deliverance was at hand.

It came about in this way: he was getting up one morning and gathering his clothes together to get dressed. But there were no socks among his clothes. He went to the bedroom door and shouted to his wife 'I can't find my . . . socks! where are the . . . things?' As he heard himself, and realized what he had just said, a great horror possessed him and he fell back on the bed in a paroxysm of despair. He cried aloud: 'O Lord, cleanse my tongue. O Lord, I can't ask for a pair of socks without swearing. Please have mercy on me and give me a clean tongue.'

As he lay there and then got up from that bed, he knew that God had done for him what he could not do for himself. His prayer, his cry of agony was heard and answered. It was his own testimony that from that moment to the end of his days no swear word or foul or blasphemous word ever again passed his lips. Hearing his own account of this amazing deliverance on a subsequent Wednesday night at the Fellowship Meeting is something that we who were there will never forget. His face, wet with tears and alight with an inner joy and wonder, his faltering voice broken with emotion, brought a warm wave of response from every heart.

He was not a speaker and I do not think that I ever heard him speak in the Fellowship Meeting either before or after that, but he would always learn some words of Scripture and repeat them as his own testimony when called upon. He was particularly drawn to the Psalms and read much in the Old Testament as well as the Gospels.

William Thomas was not what one would call a humorous character. He was heavy, sober and thoughtful but with an occasional perceptive thrust that gave the lie to any idea of lack of intelligence or emptiness.

It was his custom in the Fellowship Meeting to sit in the front row, a few feet from the raised platform where the Doctor sat. Before long he was joined there by a very different character. To this day I do not know if Mr J. had really come to a saving knowledge of the Gospel. Certain it was that something had happened to him – perhaps it was that he saw the difference that conversion had made to others, his own son among them; perhaps the approach of old age was bringing uneasiness and fears of the future; perhaps it was a strange respect he had for the Doctor and a desire to look well in his estimation. I do not know, but God knows the heart, and there remained the hope that a seed was planted and would eventually show signs of life. But at this time there was no evidence of that, except a great improvement in behaviour and demeanour and a regular attendance at all meetings.

He was small, dark and rather dirty looking, quick-brained and with a ready and rather wicked sense of humour. Because of this latter trait he was the bane of William Thomas's life. He sat close to him and would mutter comments and quips on some of the things said by others in the meeting. The old saint could not bear this attitude to the things of God – His gospel, His house, His meetings. His own attitude to all Christian things was one of loving awe. His very joy was the joy of one who had looked into hell and knew that only the love of God in Christ had saved him from it; and so he could not understand or tolerate a light spirit towards these things.

One day he had his answer ready. The muttered comments into his right ear ceased as the Doctor said, 'Have you got something to say to us, Mr Thomas?' Unhurriedly, but accompanied with a very definite 'look in the eye', the verse was repeated: 'Answer not a fool according to his folly, lest thou also be like unto him.' Truly a word in season, but it roused the rebel in old Mr J. and the next Wednesday he was as provocative as ever, if not worse. Whereupon William Thomas, in a low-pitched voice answered in what must have been a few well-chosen words, and then turned to the Doctor and recited his weekly verse: 'Answer a fool according to his folly, lest he be wise in his own conceit.' There was no more trouble from Mr J. after that!

In John Bunyan's *Pilgrim's Progress,* it was not long after losing his burden at the Cross that Christian was confronted on his journey by Apollyon in the full strength of his terrifying, evil power, and so it was with our 'pilgrim'. It was during the week following the Sunday of his first communion.

The thought that he, William Thomas, was going to join with his fellow members in the church in this act, this love feast ordained by the Lord himself, had filled all his thoughts for days, and he looked forward to this Sunday with a joy tinged with awe and humility. The Sunday came and William Thomas had his wish and joined the family of the church at the Lord's Supper. There were not many dry eyes there, and once more I was reminded of the loving joy of the natural family when the newest baby begins to walk!

It was as he sat in his house thinking over this new joy and privilege that suddenly the fiery dart of the wicked one found its target in his soul – the sun was darkened and he was fighting for his life. Out of nowhere, as it were, there was brought to his mind something that he had forgotten, from well-nigh fifty years before. Like a thunderbolt from a clear sky the incident became crystal-clear in his mind. He was a young man, and in a public house, drinking. There had been some discussion, some argument, and he, in order to gain some point, had called the Lord Jesus Christ a bastard. Now all his joy was gone, his hope was fled.

This was the dark night of his soul, the gates of Heaven were closed against him. There could be no forgiveness for this, the jaws of hell were waiting to engulf him, and he spent the long hours of that night in black despair and abject misery. 'Pilgrim' was cut down before Apollyon and lay wounded and bleeding on the ground. But now a gleam of hope entered his soul. Perhaps it was too feeble to be called hope, it was more of an overwhelming desire to share his misery with someone who would understand.

Very early that morning there was a knock at the Manse door. The unusual hour drove both the Doctor and myself to the door together. We were never likely to forget the sight that met our eyes as we opened the door.

Poor William Thomas looked as wretched, hopeless, and woeful as he felt. He came in and I left them together while he told the Doctor his pitiful story. It was no easy task to persuade him that he could be forgiven. The enormity of his sin was all he could see at first, but lovingly and patiently he was shown from the Word of God that he could indeed be forgiven and that this heinous sin, like all the others, had been washed away by the precious blood of Christ. So he was healed and restored and the dark night of his soul passed away. Peace and serenity once more ruled in his heart and joy and thankfulness for this further great release made his salvation doubly precious.

Then came a trial that threatened to rob him of much of his enjoyment in the new life. Christians have never been promised that they will not fall to the 'slings and arrows of outrageous fortune'. God has not promised his children immunity from illness and suffering – only that he will always be with them in the trial. William Thomas developed cataracts in both eyes and even after a successful operation was unable to read.

This was a bitter blow and it shook him badly. He bore it with a patience which was really wonderful in such a young Christian. There was no rebellion and no bitterness, but he was very, very sad. We all felt for him and when in a few weeks' time my own father, an eye specialist, dropped in on us on his way to West Wales, I told him about it. He was puzzled at such a result following a successful operation, and said he would be interested to see him. He found the old man's eyes in perfect condition and was convinced that all he needed was to have stronger lenses in his glasses. These he prescribed, and when the new glasses arrived William Thomas found he could read again, as well as ever and with no trouble. His joy returned and his Bible became ever more precious.

He did not have long to enjoy the 'heavenly fruits on earthly ground'. One week he was absent from the Fellowship Meeting on Wednesday night; he had caught a bad cold, they said. A day or two later a message came to the Doctor saying he was quite ill and could not be at the services. Doctor, accompanied by Mr E. T.

Rees, the church secretary, went to see him in his home.

They found the old man propped up in his bed, the little wife in anxious attendance. The first glance told all – the stertorous breathing and the high fever told their tale. He had double pneumonia – and this was before the day of modern drugs. He was far away somewhere, but responded to a greeting and a prayer. He was obviously at perfect peace and all the evidences of the old sinful, violent life were smoothed out of a now child-like face.

The minutes passed and became an hour, and more. Then suddenly the painful sound of the difficult breathing seemed to stop. The old man's face was transformed, alight, radiant. He sat up eagerly with upstretched arms and a beautiful smile on his face, as though welcoming his best of friends, and with that he was gone to that 'land of pure delight where saints immortal reign'. His church family on earth had lost for a while their aged babe – just three years old in the spiritual calendar!

EPILOGUE

Leaving Sandfields in 1938 was not easy. The memory of the Sunday-night after-meeting, at which the Minister told the congregation that the end of July would mark the conclusion of his ministry to them, is still vivid and etched indelibly on my mind. At the time it seemed unreal; I could not believe what I was hearing. And yet the call to Martyn was clear and unmistakable.

During the eleven-and-a-half years of his ministry at Sandfields there had been many invitations, often applied with some pressure, encouraging him to leave; but he had neither the slightest inclination to accept them, nor intimation that his work in Sandfields was coming to an end. But now, as he himself described it, it was as though 'a shutter had come down' and he knew that the time had come to leave our first charge. Leaving Sandfields was certainly not easy.

At the time we sensed that we were being led step by step. We did not see everything clearly, but were walking by faith. As I look back now, over the passage of the years, the guidance of God seems as clear and inevitable as a route on a map, and I marvel afresh at the way all things worked together, and at the trust and steady faith which were given to Martyn in particular. We certainly could not have realized that we were moving from eleven-and-a-half years with our church family at Sandfields to spend thirty years with our much larger church family at Westminster Chapel! In a wonderful way, our time with the first family proved to be a preparation for serving in the new family, with which Martyn's name is more usually associated.

These pages will, I hope, indicate why I am still able to thank God for the years at Sandfields, and for all the lessons we learned and friends we made there. I have recorded the stories of some of them; but eternity alone will tell the whole story.

OTHER TITLES BY OR ABOUT
DR MARTYN LLOYD-JONES
AVAILABLE FROM THE
BANNER OF TRUTH
TRUST

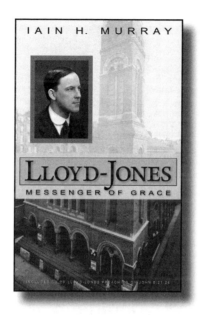

LLOYD-JONES, MESSENGER OF GRACE
ISBN 978 0 85151 975 3
288 pp. Clothbound

An important new volume on the preaching and significance of Dr Martyn Lloyd-Jones. The chapter titles include:

The Lloyd-Jones Legacies, Preaching and the Holy Spirit, The Evangelistic Use of the Old Testament, Skeletons in the Cupboard, Raising the Standard of Preaching, Lloyd-Jones and Spurgeon Compared, A Controversial Book: Joy Unspeakable, *'The Lost Leader' or 'A Prophetic Voice'?*

Includes a CD of a significant Lloyd-Jones sermon.

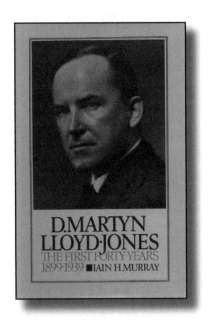

D. MARTYN LLOYD-JONES:
THE FIRST FORTY YEARS
ISBN 978 0 85151 353 9
412 pp. Clothbound

'One of the major biographies of any Christian leader of the twentieth century.'
Sword and Trowel (Australia)

'If his life were a novel it would be panned by the critics as too unrealistic . . .We are left to wonder at the providential energy that could have effected such an astonishing career.'
Christianity Today

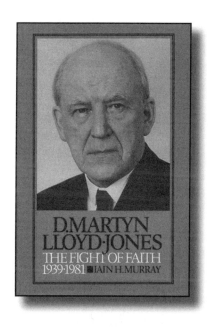

D. MARTYN LLOYD-JONES:
THE FIGHT OF FAITH
ISBN 978 0 85151 564 9
862 pp. Clothbound

'The life of Martyn Lloyd-Jones, much more than
the story of one man's life, is really the story of
evangelicalism in general and modern British
evangelicalism in particular . . . [it is] the life of a
man who will probably be viewed as the twentieth
century's most enduring and doctrinally strong
pastoral preacher.'

Trinity Journal

'Splendidly written and passes the litmus test as a good and absorbing read from a biographer completely at home and in tune.'

Methodist Recorder

'Highly recommended, especially for those hungry for those hungry for "iron rations".'

Christian Renewal

'The ministry of Martyn Lloyd-Jones at Westminster Chapel which began at the outbreak of World War 2 was suddenly changed at the point at which this volume begins. His hard work in the difficult War and post-War years became the preparation for his great influence in London in the fifties and sixties. But these pages trace his ministry into wider circles – to the Universities, to Europe, the United States, South Africa and ultimately, in his books, to the whole world. This is the second volume in a set of two. With personal experience as an assistant to Lloyd-Jones, Iain Murray gives a first hand account of one of the greatest ministries in the twentieth century. I encourage all pastors, preachers, students, and lovers of the gospel to become acquainted with Martyn Lloyd-Jones. His sermons and life will transform your mind and heart.'

Dustin Benge
Pastor and People Weblog

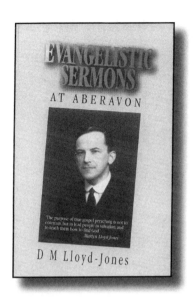

EVANGELISTIC SERMONS
AT ABERAVON
ISBN 978 0 85151 362 1
308 pp. Large Paperback

'Early examples of that "logic-on-fire" which the
author desired and commended to others. To me
their abiding value lies in the intense seriousness
of the preacher. They are worlds apart from the
triviality of so much evangelism today.'

Dick Lucas in *Churchman*

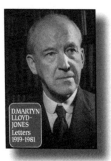

D. MARTYN LLOYD-JONES: LETTERS
1919–1981
Selected with Notes by Iain H. Murray
ISBN 978 0 85151 674 5
270 pp. Cloth-bound

'Read this book to be enriched by the depth of spiritual insight and understanding which God graciously gave to his servant . . . well-produced, lovely to handle, full of meaty subjects, with a good photograph of M.L.-J. on the dust-cover . . . worth consideration as a "gift to a friend", but put one on your own shelf first!'

Reformed Theological Journal

For more information about our publications please visit our website.

THE BANNER OF TRUTH TRUST

3 Murrayfield Road,
Edinburgh EH12 6EL
UK

P O Box 621, Carlisle,
PA 17013,
USA

www.banneroftruth.co.uk